CERTIFIED MANAGEMENT ACCOUNTANT

EXAM QUESTION & ANSWERS

A comprehensive Study guide for the management accounting certification exam, with practice test, essays, examination insights, solutions and tips.

Bruce M. Chapman

Preface

Welcome to the ultimate handbook for those planning to become Certified Management Accountants (CMAs). This painstakingly written manual is meant to be your constant companion while you strive to pass the exam. These pages contain an extensive collection of well chosen questions and answers that serve as the foundation for a strong study guide.

This book is your key to an all-encompassing learning experience; it's more than just a list of questions and answers. Our guide serves as a beacon for you as you set out on the difficult but worthwhile journey of earning your CMA certification. It provides solutions as well as a comprehensive method for understanding management accounting principles.

Explore a multitude of pieces that have been painstakingly prepared to help you better understand important concepts. Discover the nuances of management accounting through enlightening conversations and acquire a thorough understanding of the field. These pieces work as intellectual linkages, bridging the gap between theory and reality.

Real exam scenarios are the best preparation. A number of practice exams that mimic the format of the CMA certification exam are included in our guide. These exams serve as your practice run, helping you hone your time management techniques and develop the self-assurance you'll need to ace the big day.

There are obstacles on the path to success all the time, and the CMA exam is no different. You will get priceless insights into the test procedure right here, along with a road map for overcoming obstacles and seizing chances. Each question has a detailed response to help ensure that the student has a clear comprehension of the subject matter and moves toward mastery.

Achieving excellence takes strategy and dexterity in addition to knowledge. Learn tried-and-true strategies for improving your study strategy, handling exam-related stress, and performing at your best. Discover the strategies used by prosperous CMAs to set themselves apart.

Think of this handbook as your reliable ally as you work through its pages, helping you navigate the complexities of management accounting and advancing your chances of passing the CMA exam. Accept the ride, take in the information, and use this guidance as the foundation for your success on the Certified Management Accountant test.

Warmest regards on your journey to greatness.

Forward

Welcome to "Certified Management Accountant Exam: Questions & Answers," a definitive resource created with care and clarity. Set off on an adventure with an extensive study guide that has been painstakingly created to support you as you strive to succeed on the Management Accounting Certification Exam.

Our guide is your pass to success; it's more than just a list of questions and answers. Learn a plethora of information and perspectives that extend beyond traditional test-taking strategies.

Our guide's core value is our dedication to your achievement. We think it's important to give you the resources you need to succeed on your path to become a Certified Management Accountant, not just the answers. This study guide contains all the information, exercises, and strategies you need to ace the test; it's more than just a study guide.

Aim for excellence rather than merely passing. On your life-changing adventure, let "Certified Management Accountant Exam: Questions & Answers" be your guide. Armed with the information and perspectives that will make you stand out, get ready to take the test with confidence.

Introduction

In this book, You will find a variety of practice exams that have been painstakingly prepared to faithfully mirror the format and content of the actual test. These exams will familiarize you with the format of the exam as well as the different kinds of questions that you will encounter.

Additionally, the book contains detailed essay topics covering many facets of the CMA. These pieces will excite the mind and improve understanding, enabling a deeper comprehension of the topics.

Moreover, the book contains insightful assistance and crucial advice that has been handpicked from specialists who have earned remarkable test outcomes. These recommendations will offer you with a complete understanding of the exam's subject matter and the best ways to approach it.

The purpose of this book is to act as a beneficial tool to assist you pass the CMA Exam. I hope that you will perform incredibly well in your coursework and pass your tests. Remember that after you accomplish this job, success is guarantced. Starting the main course of action is the important component. We're going to get started!

TIPS FOR THE CMA EXAM:

1. Comprehend the CMA Framework: The CMA Exam revolves around the CMA framework. Make sure you have a clear understanding of the essential concepts, principles, and terminology utilized in this framework.

2. Engaging in mock exams is a great technique to familiarize oneself with the format of the exam and the different sorts of questions that will be encountered. Moreover, they can aid you in recognizing areas where you may need to increase your talents or abilities.

3. Familiarize yourself with the syllabus: Ensure that you have a full comprehension of the syllabus for the CMA Exam. This can assist you in directing your study endeavors towards the themes that are most probable to be encompassed in the examination.

4. Organize Your Time: The CMA Exam has a defined time limit. Acquire expertise in time

management to assure timely completion of all questions within the specified time span.

5. Maintain composure and concentration: It is normal to feel worried before an exam. Nevertheless, by retaining serenity and attention, you can boost your performance.

BENEFITS OF CMA EXAM

1. Global Recognition: Professionals in the fields of financial management and management accounting are given legitimacy and respect by the CMA (Certified Management Accountant) title, which is recognized worldwide.

2. Professional Growth: Passing the CMA test can lead to chances for career growth and higher-level employment. CMAs are frequently sought after by employers for positions in performance management, decision support, and strategic financial management.

3. Specialized Knowledge: The CMA test covers a wide range of subjects to guarantee that applicants gain a thorough grasp of financial planning, analysis, control, and decision support—valuable abilities that may be applied in a variety of businesses.

4. Ethical Standards: Employers and coworkers trust CMAs because they are held to a high standard of ethics. The exam places a strong emphasis on

moral issues, highlighting the value of honesty and prudent money management techniques.

5. Higher Earning Capability: When considering professionals in comparable professions who are not certified, CMAs frequently have more earning potential. The CMA test can provide candidates with specific knowledge and abilities that improve their job performance and raise their value to their employers.

1. Out of the following, which assertion regarding transfer pricing is true?

   A. Transfer price choices should never involve head office managers.

   B. The best transfer price is always going to be the market price.

   C. Divisional profits will not be impacted by the transfer price.

   D. Goal congruence should be encouraged by the transfer price

Answer : **D**

2. Which of the following choices would typically fall under the purview of a profit center manager?

i) Acquisition of non-current assets ii) Cost containment iv) Making money through sales

    A. (i), (ii) and (iii)

    B. (i) and (ii) only

    C. (i) and (iii) only

    D. (ii) and (iii) only

Answer : **D**

3. Peming Co. signed a finance lease arrangement on January 1, 2009, to acquire a machine that would have cost $166,000 if bought outright. The machine is good for six years, and the five-year lease is in effect. The machine will be returned to the lessor at the conclusion of the lease. In addition to demanding a last payment, the lease's conditions are as follows:

first-time tenant$8,000 - Rent per month, due in arrears 60 times $3,200

Implicit interest rate in lease: 8% annually

Peming allows for straight-line machinery depreciation and has a year-end of December 31.

How much of the lease agreement should be charged in the comprehensive income statement for the year ending December 31, 2009?

    A. $40,307

    B. $40,947

    C. $45,840

    D. $46,480

Answer : C

4. Which of the following descriptions of the qualities of financial information and accounting concepts is true?

A. The idea of "substance over form" states that financial statements should represent a transaction's legal meaning regardless of its economic substance.

B. Only things that can be valued monetarily are eligible for recognition in financial statements according to the historical cost concept.

C. When information is too complex for certain users to understand, it might occasionally be essential to omit it from financial statements, even though it is pertinent and trustworthy.

D. If the information is not relevant, there is no need to comply with an IAS's specific disclosure requirement.

Answer : **D**

5. Activity-based costing (ABC) is used by CMAac Co. For the upcoming year, overhead will be:

CostTotal amount spentAmount of activity

Establishment   expenses1,139,200 configurations

management of raw materialsOrders for 488,9005,000 materials

One of the company's goods is produced in 500-unit batches, requiring one setup and fifty material orders for each batch.

What is the 220 unit overhead cost using ABC?

A. $10.49

B. $453.78

C. $2,307.80

D. $5,245.00

Answer : **C**

6. Examine the following claims about activity-based costing (ABC) in the context of manufacturing:

(i) ABC does away with the volumetric approach to cost measurement.

(ii) ABC will always result in more accurate cost estimates than absorption costing.

Which combination from the list below is the right one?

 A. Statement (i) = True, Statement (ii) = True

 B. Statement (i) = False, Statement (ii) = False

 C. Statement (i) = True, Statement (ii) = False

 D. Statement (i) = False, Statement (ii) = True

        Answer : **B**

7. The following presumptions form the basis of SolutionCo's budget preparation:

Three months ended September 30, 2011: 85,720 units sold

31 December 2011: 94,560 units in three months

Inventory volume as of July 1, 2011, represented 10% of sales; as of October 1, 2011, it represented 75% of revenues for the following three months.

What is the planned volume of production for the three months ending September 30, 2011?

A. 86,383 units

B. 87,200 units

C. 84,240 units

D. 86,604 units

Answer : C

8. If cellular manufacturing is implemented as a result of a business process re-engineering initiative, which of the following scenarios is most likely to happen?

    A. Workers will acquire highly specialized skills

    B. Production runs will lengthen

    C. Control will be based on individual goals

    D. Customer value will increase

Answer : **D**

9. The following claims are relevant cost concepts to consider while making decisions:

(i) Labor can have an opportunity cost, but materials cannot.

(ii) The yearly depreciation charge is not an expense that matters.

(iii)If a decision results in a change in their overall expenditure, fixed costs would have a relevant cost element.

Which of these claims is true?

      A. (i) and (ii) only

      B. (i) and (iii) only

      C. (ii) and (iii) only

      D. (i), (ii) and (iii)

Answer : **C**

10. The online bidding will be conducted through Sun Mics' e-procurement system, which displays competing bids for each supplier. Which of the following will be a benefit of Sun Mics' e-procurement system?

A. Supply chain middlemen may be reluctant to work together out of concern that they will be cut out of the chain.

B. Investing in e-procurement would be excessively costly and hazardous.

C. Shorter lead times between putting an order and getting your delivery.

D. It would be costly and complicated to build up an integrated e-procurement system for a whole supply chain.

Answer : **C**

11. Quastir Co. produces a single item that retails for $48.80 per. The profit per unit at this selling price is $5.35 once the $65,000 in fixed costs are deducted. A production and sales volume of 20,000 units is planned.

To the closest unit, what is the margin of safety, stated in units?

    A. 7,559

    B. 7,850

    C. 12,150

    D. 12,441

Answer : **D**

12. INS Plc's receivables ledger shows a starting balance of $60,000 at the start of March 2012. A budget of $160,000 has been made aside for sales, of which 60% are expected to be paid in March following a 2.5% cash discount.

What will be the budgeted amount of receivables at the end of March if 23 percent of the opening receivables remain unpaid?

A. $76,200

B. $77,800

C. $80,200

D. $110,200

Answer : **B**

13. Out of the following, which assertion regarding transfer pricing is true?

A. The transfer price should always be determined by the market price.

B. Transfer prices enable divisions to function entirely independently

C. The complete cost should be the basis for cost-based transfer prices.

D. The purpose of using transfer prices is to draw attention to company performance

Answer : **D**

14. The analysis of Nambro's projected overheads for the upcoming year is as follows:

$1,000

Processing fees for purchase orders 450

Setup for a production run costs 180 -

Running a machine costs $640.

Over the course of the upcoming year, 32,000 hours of machine operation, 6,000 purchase orders completed, and 450 manufacturing runs are projected.

The company produces one of its items in 500-piece batches. Thirty purchase orders, 750 machine hours, and a distinct production cycle are needed for each batch.

What is the overhead cost per unit of the product using Activity Based Costing?

    A. $0.99

    B. $1.59

    C. $35.30

    D. $495.00

Answer : C

15. Revue plc employs a conventional method of costing. Labor costs for one of its items totaling $117,600 (based on four hours per unit) are included in the September budget. 3,350 units were produced in September, 150 fewer than were planned. 13,450 labor hours were worked, resulting in a labor cost of $111,850.

For the month, the labor rate variance was:

    A. $710 (F)

    B. $1,130 (F)

    C. $1,130 (A)

    D. $5,750 (A)

Answer : **B**

16. At $10, Toshi Ltd.'s selling price, a 25% markup on variable cost is achieved.

100,000 units are produced and sold annually, with $80,000 in fixed expenditures.

If costs, manufacturing, and sales volume stay the same, how much would the selling price need to rise to double profit?

    A. 12%

    B. 17%

    C. 20%

    D. 25%

Answer : **A**

17. Value for money is used by a hospital management team to evaluate performance. The surgical departments report on the following performance measures: i) The quantity of patients who require a second admission after surgery. ii) The expense of personnel for every surgery.

Which aspect of value for money does each measure evaluate?

    A. i) Economy, ii) Efficiency

    B. i) Efficiency, ii) Effectiveness

    C. i) Effectiveness, ii) Efficiency

    D. i) Effectiveness, ii) Economy

Answer : **D**

18. Which of the following claims regarding pricing strategies is true?

A. Price skimming is entering a markct with a low price at first.

B. Cost-plus pricing agreements account for the product's expected demand.

C. When competing products are similar, penetration pricing makes sense.

D. Setting a high price at first entry into a market is known as penetration pricing.

Answer : **C**

19. Bush's bank has requested that he provide an income statement that is budgeted for the six months that conclude on March 31, 2014. According to his projection, monthly sales will be $3,000 in October, $4,500 in November and December of 2013, and $5,000 starting in January of 2014.

The selling price is set to produce a 33.33% profit margin on sales.

The anticipated monthly overhead (not including depreciation) is $800. On October 1st, he intends to spend $5,000 on non-current assets. These will be paid for by the end of December, and they should last for five years, after which they will have no residual worth.

For the half-year that ends on March 31, 2014, the anticipated net profit is:

A. $3,200

B. $3,700

C. $3,950

D. $8,200

Answer : **B**

20. The value of a prepayment has been overstated, according to Repati Co.'s accountant.

When the prepayment is adjusted, how does this impact the financial statements?

A. Assets: No change, Liabilities: Reduced, CMAital: Increased

B. Assets: Increased, Liabilities: No change, CMAital: Reduced

C. Assets: Reduced, Liabilities: Reduced, CMAital: No change

D. Assets: Increased, Liabilities: No change, CMAital: Increased

Answer : **D**

21. The non-current assets of Sec Co. are being evaluated for impairment by the board in order to prepare the financial statements for the year ending October 31, 2010. They possess the following details for a certain asset:

Carrying value as of November 1, 2009$380,000

Cost of depreciation for the year ending October 31, 2010: $76,000

Market value of $285,00 - Anticipated selling expenses of $20,000.

Value in use: $250,000 - What carrying value ought to be shown in the financial situation statement as of October 31, 2010?

    A. $250,000

    B. $265,000

    C. $285,000

    D. $304,000

Answer : **B**

22. It is preferable to characterize the yearly compensation given to a company's financial accountant as follows:

   A. A variable cost.

   B. A fixed production cost.

   C. Part of prime cost.

   D. A fixed administrative cost.

Answer : **D**

23. Currently, Veetee Co. calculates the cost of one of its products as follows:

5.78 USD in direct costs - 9.38 USD in overheads (0.4 labor hours per unit)

Total cost: $15.16 - Processing and handling costs are the two categories of overhead costs, according to a cost analysis exercise. The overall cost of each activity as well as the quantity of related cost drivers are displayed in the table below.

ActivityCostCost-generating driversThe cost driver's volume

handling $17,5002,187.5 labor hours; $33,810 in handling48,300 purchase orders

For every unit produced, six purchase orders must be submitted.

What is the updated cost per unit if Activity Based Costing is implemented using the data from the cost analysis exercise as the foundation?

A. $7·40

B. $13·18

C. $14·48

D. $8·70

Answer : **B**

24. Devin Co. charges $85, the selling price of their one product. Each unit has $38 in direct expenditures and $24 in overhead. Fixed costs are recovered to the tune of 60% of overhead. The budgeted amount for both manufacturing and sales is 50,000 units.

To the nearest unit, how many units must be sold to reach the breakeven point?

    A. 14,724

    B. 19,251

    C. 25,532

    D. 31,304

Answer : **B**

25. As of May 31, 2009, Cretac Co.'s debt/equity ratio was greater than it was on May 31, 2008.

Which option below best describes the cause of the rise?

A loan that was due in 2010 has been substituted with one that is payable over the course of three years, ending in 2012.

B. A fixed-rate loan's terms have been renegotiated, and as of June 2009, the interest rate will rise.

C. The corporation bought back a number of shares in February 2009, reducing the total number of shares in circulation.

D. The shareholders approved an increase in the company's borrowing CMAacity in March 2009 in order to finance its expansion.

Answer : **C**

26. The IASB's Framework for the Preparation and Presentation of Financial Statements states that users can make predictions using information regarding an entity's liquidity and solvency.

A. The organization's potential to make money in the future.

B. The organization's CMAacity to pay its debts when they become due.

C. The allocation of future earnings and cash flows to stakeholders involved in the organization.

D. The entity's upcoming borrowing requirements.

Answer : **B**

27. Regarding target costing, which of the following propositions is/are true?

i) Once the desired cost has been determined, the features of the product are frequently determined.

ii) After the product has been launched, target costing is frequently still applied.

    A. Both (i) and (ii)

    B. (i) only

    C. (ii) only

    D. Neither (i) nor (ii)

Answer : **A**

28. Lukers Co. is organized according to its functions. The production and buying divisions are two of them. The directors hope to raise the caliber of their products and are thinking about implementing an incentive program.

Which of the following performance metrics would be a good place to start for the reward program?

A. Company profit

B. Favourable material price variances

C. Volume of products returned by customers

D. Share price

Answer : **C**

29. A product's cost gap has been measured through target costing exercises.

Which of the following actions would NOT be a suitable way to close the gap in costs?

A. Increasing the selling price of the product

B. Reducing processing times and labor input

C. Reducing the amount of packaging

D. Standardizing the components used

Answer : C

30. Calcul Co.'s divisions each produce a single item. Each unit's standard profit in one of the divisions is determined as follows:

$135 is the selling price.

Total expense of $100

$35 in profit

It is estimated that 54% of the product's overall cost is made up of fixed costs. 3,954 units are the projected production and sales quantities for the upcoming month.

What is the safety margin?

A. 39·3%

B. 43·2%

C. 56·8%

D. 60·7%

Answer : **A**

31. On the first day of the new fiscal year, the value of Vieta Co.'s non-current assets increased as a result of the directors' revaluation policy.

What effect will it have on the return on CMAital employed (ROCE) and annual net profit margin ratio of the company?

    A. ROCE = Increase, Net profit margin = Increase

    B. ROCE = Increase, Net profit margin = Decrease

    C. ROCE = Decrease, Net profit margin = Increase

    D. ROCE = Decrease, Net profit margin = Decrease

Answer : **D**

32. Dalf Co. determines the margin of safety independently for every one of its products. Here are some statistics for a single product:

Selling price ($85) for each unit

Cost per unit that varies$53 - Sales volume budgeted for 80,000 units

22% safety margin

What is the product's worth in terms of fixed costs?

    A. $3,307,200

    B. $1,996,800

    C. $2,560,000

    D. $616,000

Answer : **B**

33. Arif needs to choose which machine to buy. He has created the payout table as follows, which displays the expected income for each machine depending on demand:

minimal demand Great demand: $1,000,000.

Device A4090 -

Device B80120 -

Device C9530 -

Machine D11040: Which machine ought to be bought in accordance with the maximin criterion for making decisions?

    A. Machine A

    B. Machine B

    C. Machine C

    D. Machine D

Answer : **B**

34. Which of the following statements on the price of sales is true?

A cheap price at first introduction into the market will typically lead to market penetration.

B. Market skimming will result in a steady price over the product's life.

C. Cost plus pricing will optimize profit.

D. At the time of market entry, a target cost price will yield a profit.

Answer : **A**

35. Which goal or goals fit the bill for a transfer pricing system?

(i) Increasing company profit;

(ii) Evaluating divisional effectiveness

    A. Both (i) and (ii)

    B. (i) only

    C. (ii) only

    D. Neither (i) nor (ii)

Answer : **A**

36. For December, X's planned sales are 18,000 units. Ten percent of the production units for X are discarded as defective at the end of the process. It is planned for X to have 15,000 units of opening inventory in December and 11,400 units of closing inventory. Every finished items inventory must have passed the quality control inspection. The production budget for X in units for December is:

A. 12,960

B. 14,400

C. 15,840

D. 16,000

Answer : **D**

37. Essen Cos policy is to value inventory using the periodic weighted average method. When the financial statements were drafted, First-in, First-out (FIFO) was incorrectly used to value the closing inventory. During the period the cost of items held in inventory has fallen.

What is the effect of this error on the valuation of closing inventory and profit?

A. Inventory value = Understated, Profit = Understated

B. Inventory value = Understated, Profit = Overstated

C. Inventory value = Overstated, Profit = Overstated

D. Inventory value = Overstated, Profit = Understated

Answer : **A**

38. Financial statement items containing uncertainty should be valued using the prudential principle.

In situations of uncertainty, how does prudence impact the assessment of assets and liabilities?

A. Liabilities should be underestimated and assets inflated.

B. It is appropriate to overestimate assets and liabilities.

C. It is advisable to understate assets and liabilities.

D. It is best to overestimate liabilities and understate assets.

Answer : **D**

39. PAQ Plc produces three goods at once.

Number of units Unit of labor hours per unit

Item P1,0004:

Item A2,0006:

Q3,0003 is the product.

Total 6,000 - Overheads for the time period total $30,000. These are deducted based on labor hours.

What is the unit cost of Product A's fixed overhead?

    A. $30.00

    B. $5.00

    C. $7.20

    D. $1.20

                Answer : **D**

40. The Oken Co. sales manager is figuring out how much a prospective contract would cost. He's not sure how to figure up the opportunity cost for these two materials that are in stock right now: I Material A.Three months prior, $18,000 was spent for materials that weren't appropriate for the intended use. The items may be sold to another contractor for $7,000 if they are not used on this project. ii) Source B. This stuff is used all the time. The current inventory cost $13,000 when it was bought. These materials will need to be replaced at a cost of $15,000 if they are used for the contract.

What is the proposed contract's opportunity cost?

    A. $20,000

    B. $22,000

    C. $33,000

    D. $31,000

Answer : **B**

41. Silur Co. purchases and repairs high-end vintage jewelry. Three goods were in the company's inventory as of May 31, 2009. The goods' specifics were:

Bracelet, necklace, pendant -

Cost of purchase The anticipated selling price is $12,000,31,045,000.25,000, 38,000, and 53,000

Upfront restoration costs6,0005,0002,00

Additional expenses prior to sale Two thousand three thousand one

What was the Silurs inventory's total worth as of May 31, 2009?

A. $88,000

B. $100,000

C. $106,000

D. $107,000

Answer : B

42. Think about the following planning applications for budgets:

(i) Determine the resources required, given a particular activity level, to meet company objectives;

(ii) Prepare backup budgets, depending on fluctuating activity levels.

For these purposes, what kind of budget—fixed or flexible—is most suitable?

    A. Fixed = (i) and (ii), Flexible = neither (i) nor (ii)

    B. Fixed = (i) only, Flexible = (ii) only

    C. Fixed = (ii) only, Flexible = (i) only

    D. Fixed = neither (i) nor (ii), Flexible = (i) and (ii)

Answer : **B**

43. Which of the following descriptions of accounting principles is true?

According to the money measurement idea, financial statements can only identify elements that can be quantified in monetary terms.

According to the principle of prudence, it is preferable to overstate liabilities and understate assets when creating financial statements.

According to the historical cost principle, assets are first valued at the cost of the transaction.

(4) The "substance over form" standard states that financial statements should, if possible, show the economic substance of a transaction rather than only its legal form.

    A. 1, 2 and 3

    B. 1, 2 and 4

    C. 1, 3 and 4

    D. 2, 3 and 4

Answer : **C**

44. Which statement(s) regarding activity-based costing (ABC) is/are true?

(i) Compared to absorption costing, all product costs will be reduced under ABC.

(ii) ABC has knowledge that can help with cost-controlling.

    A. (i) only

    B. (ii) only

    C. (i) and (ii)

    D. Neither (i) nor (ii)

Answer : **B**

45. Devin Co. charges $85, the selling price of their one product. Each unit has $38 in direct expenditures and $24 in overhead. Fixed costs are recovered to the tune of 60% of overhead. The budgeted amount for both manufacturing and sales is 50,000 units.

To the closest unit, how many units are sold at the breakeven point?

    A. 14,724

    B. 19,251

    C. 25,532

    D. 31,304

Answer : **B**

46. A target costing methodology is being used by Hera Co. to design a new product. The original hypothesis was that 200,000 units could be sold for a price of $25 each, which would result in a sales volume.

However, market research suggests that the selling price should be $2350 in order to reach the sales volume of 200,000 units.

Hera wants to achieve a 20% sales profit margin on average.

For the product, the following information has been estimated:

Unit cost of direct materials: $1045 - Hourly production volume: 20 units

Hourly direct labor costs of $64. - Variable overheads$82 per hour (calculated as direct labor hours)

The projected fixed costs for producing 200,000 units are $680,000.

To reach the goal cost per unit, what decrease in cost per unit is necessary?

    A. $0.38

    B. $1.15

    C. $1.88

    D. $2.35

Answer : **D**

47. For one of the company's goods, Cambri Co.'s sales budget comprises the following sales volumes:

July: 150,900 units

August: 144,800 pieces

September: 164,800 pieces

10% of buyers, according to the sales director, will pay in the month of the transaction, and 70% will pay the following month. The remaining clients will be given an additional month's credit.

Every unit sold will be $5.50, and buyers who pay in the month of the sale will receive a 10% settlement discount.

What is the estimated amount of money that was received in September from customers for this product's sales?

A. $758,362

B. $749,298

C. $805,046

D. $814,110

Answer : **C**

48. The marketing director of Peek Co. has recommended that, in order to boost sales volume, the selling price of the product produced by one of the divisions be lowered by 3%, even though a $2 rise in variable cost per unit is predicted. At the current price of $110 per unit, the product yields a 32% contribution/sales ratio. The projected fixed costs for the upcoming year are $1,250,000.

To the closest unit, what will the breakeven sales volume be in the upcoming year?

    A. 41,806

    B. 35,511

    C. 39,062

    D. 40,323

Answer : **A**

49. Plants are depreciated by Hyginus Co. at a rate of 25% annually on a declining balance basis.

November 1, 2011 saw the purchase of a new machine. The following things were included in the invoice:

$105,000 machine

$25,000. Installation

Testing: $5,000 - Upkeep: $6,000 for a full year ending on October 31, 2012

What entire amount of the machine's cost should be deducted from profit for the year ending October 31, 2012?

    A. $35,250

    B. $62,250

    C. $33,750

    D. $39,750

                  Answer : **D**

50. Deyal Co. will gain money later on as a result of a transaction being completed.

Which of the following financial statement items needs to be acknowledged right now?

A. Income

B. Equity

C. Asset

D. Liability

Answer : **C**

51. Give an explanation of cost accounting and its function in management accounting.

_____

_____

_____

_____

_____

_____

_____

_____

_____

_____

52. What distinguishes activity-based costing from conventional costing techniques?

_____

_____

_____

_____

_____

_____

_____

_____

_____

_____

_____

53. Talk about the idea of budgeting and how crucial it is to management accounting.

_____

_____

_____

_____

_____

_____

_____

_____

_____

_____

_____

54. Describe the distinction between variable and fixed expenses and give instances of both.

_____

_____

_____

_____

_____

_____

_____

_____

_____

_____

_____

55. Outline the procedures for doing variance analysis and standard pricing.

_____

_____

_____

_____

_____

_____

_____

_____

_____

_____

_____

56. Talk about how important cost-volume-profit (CVP) analysis is for making managerial decisions.

_____

_____

_____

_____

_____

_____

_____

_____

_____

_____

57. Describe how responsibility accounting is used to assess the performance of organizations.

_____

_____

_____

_____

_____

_____

_____

_____

_____

_____

58. Explain and contrast marginal and absorption costing.

_____

_____

_____

_____

_____

_____

_____

_____

_____

_____

_____

59. Talk about the idea of relevant costing and how it can be used to make decisions.

_____

_____

_____

_____

_____

_____

_____

_____

_____

_____

_____

60. What are the implications of transfer pricing for international companies, and what are some possible countermeasures?

_____

_____

_____

_____

_____

_____

_____

_____

_____

_____

61. Describe the balanced scorecard idea and how it relates to performance evaluation.

_____

_____

_____

_____

_____

_____

_____

_____

_____

_____

_____

62. Talk about the benefits and drawbacks of decentralization in terms of organizational structure.

_____

_____

_____

_____

_____

_____

_____

_____

_____

_____

63. In a manufacturing setting, define and distinguish between direct and indirect expenses.

_____

_____

_____

_____

_____

_____

_____

_____

_____

_____

64. Examine how inflation affects management choices and financial statements.

_____

_____

_____

_____

_____

_____

_____

_____

_____

_____

_____

65. Describe economic value added (EVA) and how it's used to assess performance.

_____

_____

_____

_____

_____

_____

_____

_____

_____

_____

_____

66. Talk on how management accounting procedures incorporate ethical issues.

_____

_____

_____

_____

_____

_____

_____

_____

_____

_____

_____

67. Describe the idea of the "cost of quality" and how it affects companies.

_____

_____

_____

_____

_____

_____

_____

_____

_____

_____

_____

68. Examine risk management's significance in relation to management accounting.

_____

_____

_____

_____

_____

_____

_____

_____

_____

_____

69. Talk on the importance of sustainability and environmental accounting in contemporary company.

_____

_____

_____

_____

_____

_____

_____

_____

_____

_____

_____

70. Describe target costing and how it is used to determine prices.

_____

_____

_____

_____

_____

_____

_____

_____

_____

_____

_____

71. List the essential components of a master budget and explain how it fits into the planning process.

_____

_____

_____

_____

_____

_____

_____

_____

_____

_____

72. Talk on how technology has affected management accounting procedures.

_____

_____

_____

_____

_____

_____

_____

_____

_____

_____

73. Describe relevant range and its importance in the analysis of cost behavior.

74. Use break-even analysis to examine how cost, volume, and profit are related to one another.

_____

_____

_____

_____

_____

_____

_____

_____

_____

_____

_____

75. Talk about the benefits and drawbacks of outsourcing from the standpoint of management accounting.

_____

_____

_____

_____

_____

_____

_____

_____

_____

_____

76. Describe and distinguish between the methodologies of direct and absorption costing.

_____

_____

_____

_____

_____

_____

_____

_____

_____

_____

_____

77. Talk about how management accounting affects the way strategic decisions are made.

_____

_____

_____

_____

_____

_____

_____

_____

_____

_____

_____

78. Describe the idea of job order costing and how manufacturing sectors use it.

_____

_____

_____

_____

_____

_____

_____

_____

_____

_____

_____

79. Examine how globalization has affected management accounting procedures.

_____

_____

_____

_____

_____

_____

_____

_____

_____

_____

80. Talk about the benefits and guiding principles of just-in-time (JIT) inventory management.

_____

_____

_____

_____

_____

_____

_____

_____

_____

_____

_____

81. Describe the idea of cost behavior and how it affects managerial choices.

_____

_____

_____

_____

_____

_____

_____

_____

_____

_____

82. Talk about the significance of variance analysis in assessing performance.

_____

_____

_____

_____

_____

_____

_____

_____

_____

_____

83. Examine how management accounting is used to assess investment initiatives.

_____

_____

_____

_____

_____

_____

_____

_____

_____

_____

84. Describe the distinctions between management and financial accounting.

_____

_____

_____

_____

_____

_____

_____

_____

_____

_____

85. Talk about the opportunities and difficulties involved in putting activity-based costing into practice.

_____

_____

_____

_____

_____

_____

_____

_____

_____

_____

_____

86. Explain and go over the idea of applicable costs in situations when decisions need to be made.

_____

_____

_____

_____

_____

_____

_____

_____

_____

_____

87. Describe the fundamentals of responsibility accounting and how organizational control uses it.

_____

_____

_____

_____

_____

_____

_____

_____

_____

_____

_____

88. Examine how management accounting techniques are affected by regulatory compliance.

_____

_____

_____

_____

_____

_____

_____

_____

_____

_____

89. Talk about how management accountants promote the sustainability of their organizations.

_____

_____

_____

_____

_____

_____

_____

_____

_____

_____

90. Describe the idea of throughput accounting and how production settings use it.

_____

_____

_____

_____

_____

_____

_____

_____

_____

_____

_____

91. Examine how cost allocation functions in the service sector.

_____

_____

_____

_____

_____

_____

_____

_____

_____

_____

92. Talk about the value of benchmarking in evaluating performance.

_____

_____

_____

_____

_____

_____

_____

_____

_____

_____

_____

93. Describe the idea of cost control and how budgetary management uses it.

_____

_____

_____

_____

_____

_____

_____

_____

_____

_____

_____

94. Talk about the benefits and drawbacks of standard expenses in management accounting.

_____

_____

_____

_____

_____

_____

_____

_____

_____

_____

_____

95. Examine how risk and return are related when making investing decisions.

_____

_____

_____

_____

_____

_____

_____

_____

_____

_____

96. Describe the idea of process costing and how continuous production environments use it.

_____

_____

_____

_____

_____

_____

_____

_____

_____

_____

97. Talk about the moral issues surrounding performance reviews and budgeting.

_____

_____

_____

_____

_____

_____

_____

_____

_____

_____

98. Examine how dynamic pricing techniques affect management accounting.

_____

_____

_____

_____

_____

_____

_____

_____

_____

_____

99. Explain and go over the idea of relevant range as it relates to cost behavior analysis.

_____

_____

_____

_____

_____

_____

_____

_____

_____

_____

_____

100. Talk about how strategic cost management uses management accounting.

_____

_____

_____

_____

_____

_____

_____

_____

_____

_____

_____

Made in the USA
Las Vegas, NV
30 April 2024

89329107R00066